WELCOME

TO

EVERGLADES

NATIONAL PARK

A Fun and Affordable Adventure to Gators, Glades, and Beyond

ANGELINA GUTHRIE

Everglades National Park Travel Guide 2024

© 2024 Angelina Guthrie

TABLE OF CONTENTS

MAP OF EVERGLADES NATIONAL PARK

INTRODUCTION

Welcome to Everglades National Park, the wild and untamed environment in southern Florida, United States of America. An unforgettable excursion awaits amid the broad landscapes of marshes, mangroves, and sawgrass meadows. As you hold this handbook in your hands, prepare to discover the many charms of one of America's most appealing national parks.

Imagine an endless expanse of stunningly magnificent countryside, with emerald-colored streams shimmering in the sun's golden rays. Excitement fills the air, bringing with it the fragrances of distant flowers and the promise of thrilling discovery. Everglades National Park offers a gastronomic experience that will have your taste buds dancing, from tantalizing seafood shacks to hidden gems serving regional delicacies.

Even more than its culinary offers, Everglades National Park is distinguished by its amazing biodiversity. The eyes of ancient reptiles peer out from the darkness, reminding us of the park's wilder side. Do not be scared; we will take you on safe excursions with these beautiful creatures, ensuring that you witness their majesty and beauty from a respectful distance.

As you tour the park's many ecosystems, keep an eye out for avian wonders with beautiful colors. Everglades National Park is a birdwatcher's paradise, home to over 350 distinct species. Each sighting, from the majestic great blue heron to the sociable roseate spoonbill, demonstrates the park's commitment to biodiversity conservation.

You could be considering staying since there are opportunities to see fantastic happenings at every turn. Travelers need not fear, since Everglades National Park offers a range of options to meet the needs of all adventure enthusiasts. After each day of exploration, you can be certain that warmth and quiet await you, whether in modest lodges nestled in the forests or rustic campers under the stars.

So, when you go into the heart of Everglades National Park, dear reader, let this guide serve as your map, your storyteller, and your reliable journey partner. Discover the secrets of this amazing wilderness; enjoy the joys of its gourmet offers; marvel at the majesty of its alligators; and immerse yourself in the symphony of bird songs.

Having this guide with you will guarantee that your journey to Florida's southernmost point, Everglades National Park, is nothing short of fantastic. Now plunge in, explore, and be captivated by the splendor of this natural paradise. There is an adventure coming!

A Brief History of Everglades

Imagine visiting a region that hasn't changed in thousands of years, where gator cries reverberate through time and sawgrass whispers stories of vanished cultures. Greetings from Everglades National Park, where visitors may enjoy not just a magnificent scenery but also a dynamic mosaic with a fascinating history to learn.

As you stand in the park's lush center, you may be able to see its origin tale unfold in front of you.

When drainage operations affected the Everglades' underlying structure and plume hunters killed bird populations in the late 1800s, it looked that paradise had vanished. Enter visionaries like Marjory Stoneman Douglas, whose unwavering voice sparked a conservation movement that resulted in the park's formation in 1934.

Explore Shark Valley's paths, which were formerly used by Seminole Indians who had lived in the Everglades for many years. Consider their boats floating down rivers, their life in harmony with the pulse of the earth. Stand at the Flamingo Visitor Center to honor the young men who battled the Civilian Conservation Corps with shovels and saplings rather than guns to restore the Everglades' delicate balance.

However, the narrative is not yet over. Every rustling of sawgrass symbolizes the continuing conservation struggle. As you see ongoing restoration efforts, you will realize how committed the human spirit is to protecting this unique ecosystem.

The Everglades is more than simply a vacation destination; it's a living museum where you can learn about the region's history, see its present difficulties, and even help shape its future. When you go on your quest, keep in mind that you are a storyteller carrying on the heritage of those who battled to preserve this unique gem. Thus, pay great attention because the Everglades are whispering its past, waiting for you to discover its secrets and join in its enthralling narrative.

Weather and Climate

Imagine waking up to the sound of cicadas, sunshine peeking through the knees of cypress trees, and the promise of adventure shimmering in the morning mist. Welcome to the Everglades, where the weather adds a unique twist to your tropical getaway, mirroring the diversity of the surroundings.

Embrace the Dance of Seasons:

- **Dry Season (Dec-Apr):** Airboat rides and wildlife treks are best enjoyed on sunny days. Don't let the odd front or chilly night deceive you; instead, prepare by packing layers of clothing. It is, after all, Florida's dry season, not an arid one, so humidity will be hanging about like a nosy acquaintance.
- **Wet Season (May-Nov):** Get ready for an amazing tropical event! Afternoon

thunderstorms release their ferocity, leaving puddles brimming with life and the air electrified with electricity. It's the best time of year to see animals, but be prepared with rain gear and be aware that mosquitoes may join the fun.

A Word on the Wild:

- **Hurricane Season (June-Nov):** Observe weather predictions, however they are seldom. Postpone your excursion if a storm is forecast. We assure you that you do not want to get tangled up with a gator in a deluge, even if the park shuts for safety during storms.
- **Sunshine is King:** Sun protection is always your best friend. The Florida heat doesn't discriminate, so bring a hat, sunglasses, and sunscreen.

Beyond the Forecast:

Although the weather in the Everglades may appear erratic, it is really one of its charms. It serves as a reminder that you are traveling through a live, breathing ecosystem rather than in a controlled space. Savor the unexpected, the cool showers, the warm nights with fireflies, and the sun-filled mornings full of opportunities for exploration.

The Everglades are an experience, not simply a location, so keep that in mind. You'll return with memories carved in sunlight and recollections that won't be wiped away by any rainfall if you let the weather contribute its own special chapter to your experience.

Top Reasons to Visit Everglades

Picture a place where shadows dance in cypress swamps, old giants relax in the sun, and there is fun around every corner. That's the Everglades National Park, where a vibrant patchwork of habitats guarantees an unforgettable experience. What distinguishes this park, other from its beautiful surroundings? Here are the main reasons why you should plan your next holiday to the Everglades, so take your seat, nature lover.

1. Unique Ecosystem: Explore the largest subtropical wilderness in the United States, home to diverse wildlife and plants, including mangrove forests, sawgrass marshes, and cypress swamps.

2. Wildlife Encounters: Spot alligators, crocodiles, birds, turtles, fish, and numerous other species in their natural habitats, including the endangered Florida panther and manatee.

3. Airboat Tours: Experience the thrill of gliding across the marshy grasslands on an airboat, providing an unforgettable perspective on the Everglades' vast expanse.

4. Hiking and Camping: Discover scenic trails and campsites for a deeper connection with nature, including the 99-mile Wilderness Waterway and backcountry sites.

5. Kayaking and Canoeing: Paddle through tranquil waters and get up close to wildlife, exploring the Everglades' intricate network of rivers, lakes, and wetlands.

6. Birdwatching: Witness an incredible array of bird species, including herons, egrets, eagles, ospreys, and numerous migratory birds.

7. Cultural Significance: Learn about the history and traditions of the indigenous Miccosukee and Seminole tribes, who have lived in harmony with the Everglades for centuries.

8. Scientific Research: Visit the Everglades as a living laboratory for scientific discovery and conservation, with numerous research centers and initiatives.

9. Outdoor Adventures: Enjoy fishing, boating, photography, and stargazing in a breathtaking setting, with opportunities for both relaxation and excitement.

10. Preservation Efforts: Support conservation initiatives and experience the importance of protecting this fragile ecosystem, which provides vital habitat for countless species.

11. Year-Round Events: Participate in festivals, guided walks, educational programs, and seasonal celebrations, such as the Everglades City Seafood Festival.

12. Accessibility: Explore the Everglades via convenient locations near Miami, Fort Lauderdale, Naples, and other South Florida cities.

13. Diverse Landscapes: Encounter a range of landscapes, from the sawgrass prairies to the mangrove forests, cypress swamps, and pine rocklands.

14. Seasonal Changes: Witness the Everglades' transformation throughout the year, with changing water levels, wildlife migrations, and blooming vegetation.

15. Adventure and Relaxation: Combine thrilling outdoor activities with serene natural beauty, making the Everglades an ideal destination for both adventure-seekers and those seeking relaxation.

Pack your camera, your spirit of adventure, and your reverence for the natural world. The Everglades is waiting, eager to create lifelong memories. Recall that this isn't just a trip; it's a chance to join the narrative that this untamed and beautiful location is creating.

Planning Your Everglades Adventure

Choosing Your Entrance Point

Though it might be difficult to decide whether to enter its lush embrace, the Everglades whispers tales of excitement. Do not be scared, intrepid adventurer—each doorway leads to a new experience!

Start your classic Everglades adventure at Homestead. Take a tram ride across sawgrass meadows, search for sun-lounging alligators, and learn about the park's history in the Ernest F. Coe Visitor Center. This is the best starting place for families and anybody searching for traditional Everglades experiences.

Gulf Coast: Show off your wild side! Cast your line for a snook in the clear seas, kayak through vibrant mangrove mazes, and discover the Ten Thousand Islands, an intricate network of islands full of mysteries. This is for the daring spirit looking for unspoiled beauty and off-the-beaten-path discovery.

Flamingo: Venture far into the heart of the Everglades. Trek through bird-filled cypress swamps, discover isolated islands reachable by boat, and take in the magnificent sunsets from the Flamingo Visitor Center. This is for the person who loves to be by themselves and in calm connection with the unadulterated beauty of nature.

But wait! There's more:

- Are you a time traveler? Easy access to Miami's Art Deco treasures is provided via Homestead.
- A Beach Commie? Incorporate days of sunshine in Naples, close to the Gulf Coast entry, with your Everglades exploration.
- Are you worried about your budget? While Homestead has greater hotel options, Flamingo and Gulf Coast both provide camping.

So which whispers speak to you, dear explorer? One remarkable chapter at a time, let the Everglades reveal its charm to you by selecting your doorway. Recall that the trip, the decisions you make, and the tales you create deep inside this wild paradise are what constitute an adventure, not simply the final destination.

Best Time to Visit

The Everglades calls all year long with its patchwork of green lakes and whispering sawgrass. So when should you answer the phone? To choose your perfect season, let's interpret the cues from the weather and wildlife:

Dry Season Symphony (December - April):

- **Sunshine's Embrace:** Enjoy mild weather that is ideal for nature hikes and airboat excursions. Although evenings in Florida might be chilly, wear layers since humidity persists even during the "dry" season.

- **Gator Gala:** These ancient behemoths may be seen soaking in the sun; they are more common in the warmer months.

- **Festivals and Frolicking:** Take part in colorful occasions such as the Everglades Seafood Festival or see amusing manatees congregating in warmer waters.

Wet Season Spectacle (May - November):

- **Nature's Theatrics:** Witness the stunning afternoon thunderstorms that change the environment and elicit behavior from wildlife.

- **Birding Bonanza:** Birdwatchers will find heaven during this season, which is bursting at the seams with feathered guests. As you are ready to be astounded, pack your binoculars.
- **Mosquito Masquerade:** Recall that these buzzing friends are brought by rain. Wear light, long-sleeved clothes and bring bug repellant.

Beyond the Seasons:

- **Hurricane Heed:** The season for hurricanes runs from June to November. Although unusual, pay attention to weather reports and reschedule if necessary.
- **Summer Sizzle:** July and August can be extraordinarily hot and muggy. For outdoor activities, take into consideration the early mornings and nights.

Choosing Your Adventure:

- Do You Watch Wildlife? When animals are more visible, choose the dry season.
- Photographer of nature subjects? Rich foliage and striking sky are features of the rainy season.
- Budget Traveler? Lower prices and nicer weather are available during shoulder seasons (May/June, October/November).

Keep in mind that the Everglades are an ecosystem that is alive and well. Accept the weather as a part of the journey, and when it passes, you'll have memories imprinted in the ever-shifting moods of nature as well as sunlight.

Getting to Everglades

There are various routes to get to Everglades National Park, making it easy for visitors to explore this spectacular natural location. Driving is one of the most convenient ways to get to the park. Because main roads link to the park's gates, driving allows you to explore it at your leisure.

People who choose to travel in a more environmentally responsible manner can use public transit. Miami-Dade Transit operates bus services that connect Miami and its surrounding areas to Everglades National Park. With this affordable option, guests may unwind and enjoy the gorgeous journey.

A guided boat ride is a fantastic opportunity to explore the park's waterways. These carefully led tours provide a new perspective on the Everglades' intricate ecology and showcase its breathtaking beauty.

Biking is a popular mode of transportation in the park for those who dare. Riding a bike through the Everglades provides an intimate and up-close interaction with nature, as designated paths and bike rentals are available.

Thus, airboat tours are an exciting choice for thrill enthusiasts. Passengers in these flat-bottomed boats may expect an exciting voyage as competent captains navigate the wetlands. The boats go smoothly across the water.

Regardless of which method of transportation you choose, the trip to Everglades National Park is thrilling and creates the ideal ambiance for an unforgettable experience.

Accommodations & Camping Options

The Everglades is more than just a park; it's an escape, and how you remain dictates the path of your adventure. As a result, instead of generic housing options, consider unique options that embody the spirit of the wild:

For the Rustic Soul:

- **Campgrounds:** Set up camp at Flamingo or Long Pine Key under a blanket of stars. Get up to the sound of birdsong, have dinner outside, and take in the untainted beauty of the Everglades. Keep in mind that there aren't many amenities at these campgrounds, so bring light.

- **Lodges & Cabins:** Flamingo Lodge or Everglades National Park Lodges provide comfortable, rustic-chic accommodations. Relish the comforts of home, such as air conditioning and restrooms, in the company of nature. Ideal for anyone looking for adventure mixed with comfort.

For the Glamping Guru:

- **Eco-Tents:** Enjoy the outdoors without compromising luxury in these stylish eco-tents provided by private businesses close to the park. Savor comforts like air conditioning, cozy mattresses, and private decks while taking in the Everglades' atmosphere.

- **Glamping Locations:** Upgrade your camping experience with opulent features like hot tubs, separate toilets, and even glamping platforms at glamping locations close to the park. Savor the excitement of being outside while adding a little luxury.

For the Family Funseeker:

- **Vacation Rentals:** Near the park entrance, look for a large house or a quaint cabin with many bedrooms, kitchens, and even private pools. Ideal for families looking for convenience, room, and the ability to prepare their own meals.

- **Resorts:** Choose resorts like those in Homestead or Naples that are not inside the park. Take advantage of the convenient proximity to the Everglades for day outings, along with facilities like restaurants, swimming pools, and scheduled activities.

Beyond the Basics:

- **Take into account your demands for accessibility:** Be sure to check the campground's accessibility before making a reservation.

- **Reserve ahead of time:** Popular choices tend to sell out fast, especially at the busiest times of year.
- **Evaluate your schedule:** Select a lodging that will accommodate your schedule of events and your preference for being close to certain park entrances.

Whatever your taste, the Everglades offer a unique journey starting point, focusing on soaking in its distinctive ambience and creating lasting memories. Make wise decisions and bring your spirit of adventure.

Hotels Near Everglades National Park

1. Super 8 by Wyndham (3 stars): Everglades adventure meets affordable luxury. Steps away from the park, you wake up to the sound of chirping birds.

Take advantage of the spotless accommodations, cool pool, and helpful staff who are eager to help you explore. From $80 for three nights.

2. Travelodge by Wyndham (3 stars): Your gateway to accessibility and exploration. Large, comfortable rooms with free WiFi, nice beds, and a handy position close to the park entrance. Following a day of exploration, unwind by the pool. From $90 for three nights.

3. Best Western Gateway To The Keys (3 stars): Add a little of Everglades charm while embracing the Keys feel. Large, balcony-equipped rooms, a dazzling pool, and on-site restaurants are available. Visit the park or the neighboring beaches. $120 for three nights.

4. Fisher Inn Resort & Marina (4 stars): Take in the embrace of nature. Private balconies, access to the marina, and an on-site restaurant characterize this waterfront paradise. Fish, go on guided trips, or kayak through mangroves. Stays for three nights starting at $150.

Note: Depending on the season and availability, prices may differ from what is estimated.

Restaurants and Cafes in Everglades

1. Villagio Restaurant & Bar: Think about enjoying brilliant seafood and tropical drinks while sitting on a colorful terrace with a view of the water. Delicious food, a laid-back vibe, and attentive service are what make Villagio so charming. Enjoy Key West staples like coconut shrimp ($18) and their famous lobster bisque ($22). It's the ideal getaway after a day in the Everglades, complete with live music and breathtaking sunsets.

2. Park & Ocean: A farm-to-table experience with an emphasis on seasonal, local foods is provided by Park & Ocean, which is tucked away within beautiful vegetation. Savor their mouthwatering pan-seared scallops ($28) or treat yourself to a gourmet burger ($20) made with grass-fed cattle. Park & Ocean is a visual and culinary delight, emphasizing sustainability while offering stunning vistas.

3. Celebration Park Naples: At Celebration Park, take in all of Naples' colorful vitality. A variety of food choices are available in this outdoor space, including delicious tacos ($12) at Cantina Laredo and superb sushi rolls ($15) at Tsunami. The Brass Pelican ($8) offers specialty beers and live music in a vibrant ambiance that's ideal for celebrating after an adventure.

4. Kapow Noodle Bar: Near the Everglades, are you craving something Asian? The Kapow Noodle Bar is excellent! Taste their delicious ramen bowls ($14), indulge in their famous pad thai ($16), or peruse their extensive menu of Vietnamese delicacies. Kapow Noodle Bar is a tasty stop for any traveler, offering prompt service and a laid-back atmosphere.

Remember: Prices are estimates and may vary depending on the season and menu choices.

There's a gastronomic treasure close to the Everglades waiting to be found, regardless of your preferences or price range. Set off on your journey and enjoy the tastes that go well with the marvels of this distinct ecology!

Essential Gear & Packing Tips

Ready to head to the Everglades? The following items are essential for creating a journey to remember:

Water and Sun Warrior:

- **Shades with a sun hat:** The sun in Florida is really intense. Bring polarized sunglasses and a hat with a broad brim for the best possible protection.

- **Reusable filter-equipped water bottle:** Purify your own water to stay hydrated and save the environment. Extra points for having insulation!

- **Clothes that dry quickly and layers:** Be prepared for high humidity and erratic rains. To adapt to temperature variations, bring layers of clothing that are breathable and moisture-wicking.

Bug Busters:

- **Insect repellent:** To get the most protection against mosquitoes and other bothersome insects, choose an insect repellent that contains DEET.
- **Long sleeves with a thin long sleeve shirt:** Cover exposed skin, especially at dawn and twilight when mosquito activity is at its highest.
- **First-aid box:** Carry necessities such as sting relief, antiseptic wipes for small cuts and bites, and antihistamines.

Adventure Awaits:

- **Hiking Shoes:** Wear comfortable hiking shoes to explore terrain that provide enough ankle support and traction. If it's raining, wear shoes that can withstand the elements.
- **Waterproof backpack:** A waterproof backpack will shield your belongings from unexpected downpours.

- **Binoculars and camera:** Take in the splendor of the Everglades' natural environments and fauna.
- **Dry bag:** Protect your belongings from water while on a boat excursion or from unforeseen spills.

Bonus Tips:

- **Obtain offline map downloads:** With offline maps on your phone, you can prevent getting lost in the woods.
- **Don't overpack, but do bring necessities:** Pack only what you'll need for the activities you have planned and give priority to lightweight items.
- **Be mindful of the surroundings:** To protect this special habitat, leave no trace and abide by park rules.

Do not forget that this is only the beginning. Make sure your packing list reflects your unique itinerary, length of stay, and personal tastes. Enjoy a fantastic trip to the Everglades!

Permits, Fees, and Regulations

Though the Everglades may greet you with open arms and even a few inquisitive gators, keep in mind that it's a fragile environment with its own set of regulations. Before you go, make sure you know these things:

Permits:

- **Backcountry Camping:** A permit is required for overnight stays outside of licensed campgrounds if you're looking for privacy beneath the stars. Apply far in advance, especially if it's the busiest time of year.
- **Special Activities:** Permits are needed for kayaking beyond approved zones, commercial filming, and giving guided tours. For specifics, speak with the park service.

- **Fishing:** Both freshwater and saltwater fishing in the park require a license. Keep in mind catch limitations and seasonal rules.

Entrance Fees:

- **Park Entrance:** To access the park, one must have a valid day or yearly pass. Think about getting a multi-day pass if you want to do a lot of exploration.

- **Guided excursions:** Keep in mind that many excursions have additional costs, so plan accordingly.

- **Boat rentals:** Renting an airboat, a kayak, or a canoe is frequently required. For popular tours, weigh your alternatives and make reservations in advance.

Regulations:

- **Remain on the Trail:** Adhere to prescribed routes in order to preserve the delicate environment and prevent upsetting wildlife.

- **Leave No Trace:** Empty the park of all waste, have as little influence as possible, and leave it in its original state.
- **Wildlife Encounters:** Keep a safe distance when observing animals. Don't feed them, ignore them, or impede their instincts.
- **Respect Cultural Sites:** Recognize the importance of historical and cultural sites to the park's past and treat them with regard.

Pro Tip: Get the most recent information on fees, permits, rules, and even virtual tours given by rangers by downloading the National Park Service app. Your Everglades excursion may be sustainable and wonderful with a little planning and courtesy!

Must-See Sights and Activities

Alligators, Manatees & Diverse Wildlife

Life abounds in the Everglades National Park, where visitors may have remarkable interactions with a wide range of personalities. Prepare for:

Witness the Throne of the Gator: Keep an eye out for the alligator, who reigns supreme over the swamp. Take a boat excursion through the mangroves and glide gently across the river, seeing these ancient giants sunning themselves or gracefully gliding through the water. Recall to honor their territory; keep a safe distance and don't disrupt their tranquility.

Swim with the Gentle Giants: Meet the gentle giants of Florida's waters, the manatees, sometimes known as "sea cows." A special chance to see their graceful, serene movements while feeding on submerged flora is provided by kayaking excursions. Keep in mind that these gentle giants should be treated with care and that it is important not to disturb their vital feeding places.

Birdwatching Paradise: Everglades National Park is a birdwatcher's paradise. Marvel at the anhingas' amazing feats of balance, be enthralled by the colorful roseate spoonbills, and hear the eerie cries of the sandhill cranes. The air becomes a symphony of color and melody as each turn reveals a new feathered beauty.

Beautiful Slitherers: Don't let the odd slither worry you! Although there are some poisonous snakes in the Everglades, innocuous snake species like the Eastern diamondback water snake and the multicolored rat snake are more prevalent. Recognize their special place in the ecology by keeping a safe distance from them.

Beyond the Big Names: The Everglades' hidden treasures are what really make them magical. See alligators that resemble dinosaurs snapping turtles, observe otters having fun on the banks, or take in the vivid butterflies flying through the cypress woods. Each interaction, regardless of size, enriches the fabric of this distinct ecology.

Keep in mind that respect is essential. Never go near, feed, or bother animals. Keep a safe distance and permit them to carry out their instinctive actions. To improve your experience and learn the names of the wonderful animals you see, download a wildlife identification app.

A chance to interact with nature's beauties and make lifelong memories awaits you at every turn in the Everglades, so get ready to be enthralled.

Exploring Diverse Ecosystems

The Everglades is a patchwork of distinct habitats that each provide a window into a different world; it is more than simply a swamp. Prepare to investigate:

Sawgrass Prairies: Picture a huge, undulating sea of golden grass that is waving in the wind. From secretive bobcats to elegant wading birds like herons and egrets, this famous habitat is brimming with life. Experience the vastness of this natural marvel by going on a tram trip or hiking via secret routes.

Cypress Swamps: Enter a mysterious world covered with Spanish moss. With its twisted roots producing a maze-like environment, towering cypress trees rise out of the water. Paddle across these peaceful streams in a kayak, seeing basking turtles and taking in the eerie barred owl sounds at nightfall.

Mangrove Forests: Explore the colorful environment where land and sea converge. Mangrove roots twist to create a labyrinth above the sea that serves as a haven for fish, crabs, and occasionally even manatees. Cruise about in a boat, taking in the beautiful dance of land and sea, and be amazed at how resilient these unusual ecosystems are.

Tropical Hardwood Hammocks: Find shade under a lush hardwood hammock to avoid the sun's glare. Set among vibrant birds such as the elusive Florida panther and entertaining raccoons, towering trees covered in vines offer a refreshing break from the heat. Trek these colorful islands and you'll feel as though you've traveled to a tropical haven in the middle of the huge Everglades.

Marine and Estuarine Waters: Explore the Everglades' marine and estuarine waters to discover their life. Kayak through dazzling waters to see playful dolphins and inquisitive manatees. While snorkeling in pure waters, you'll see a variety of species and spectacular coral reefs. Observe the delicate balance that exists between fresh and saltwater—a key nursery for a diverse array of marine life.

Keep in mind that each ecosystem is a precious gem. Respect and abide by the park's guidelines to ensure the survival of its diverse population. The Everglades will unveil its secrets to you if you allow your curiosity lead you, providing you with lifelong memories.

Shark Valley Tram Tours

See the famous Everglades grassland unfolding before you as you glide across a sea of sawgrass. This is how the Shark Valley Tram Tour works; it takes you on a singular adventure right into the center of this amazing environment.

Take a ride on the open-air tram and discover the Everglades' mysteries with the knowledgeable guide. Views of sun-loving alligators serve as a continual reminder of the wilderness surrounding you. See wading birds, such as egrets and herons, as their elegant shapes soar into the vivid blue sky. The excitement of the chase is increased by finding hidden treasures like playful otters and elusive bobcats.

The tram makes stops at viewpoints with jaw-dropping views as it travels deeper. Take in a 360-degree panorama of the Everglades, a huge green and blue canvas, by scaling the Shark Valley Observation Tower. Use your camera to capture the event, but keep in mind that taking it all in is what will make it truly magical.

The trip offers an educational experience as well as a sightseeing excursion. Discover the complex ecological balance, the continuing conservation efforts, and the risks that this important region is facing. Go from the Everglades with a renewed respect for its wonders and a resolve to preserve them.

Renting a bike following the tram excursion will improve your experience. Discover undiscovered paths at your own speed as you venture more into the woods, enjoying the sun and breeze in your hair.

Shark Valley Tram Tours provide a doorway to an incredible journey rather than merely a ride. So grab a seat, let your senses wander, and be ready to be astounded by the Everglades' core.

Airboat Rides

Hold on tightly! Fasten your seatbelts for a thrilling voyage across the Everglades aboard a fearsome airboat. These beautiful, fan-powered boats provide an adrenaline rush unlike any other, so forget about a relaxing boat ride.

Think of yourself riding in an airboat over sawgrass fields, the wind whipping through your hair as you go. The splash of water may be felt as you pass through cypress tunnels and huge trees form a majestic archway above. Look for creatures; as you go closer, frightened birds may take flight, and alligators may be sunning on the banks.

Aside from being speedy, the airboat excursion is also instructive. From rare flora and insects to elusive species like otters and turtles, your skilled guide will point out hidden gems. Learn more about the Everglades' delicate natural balance and the need of maintaining this critical wetland.

Remember the joy, though! Experience the thrill of precise movements as your skillful captain expertly directs the airboat. Take pictures to remember the event, but most importantly, experience the exhilaration and pure splendor of the Everglades.

Choose an early morning or late afternoon journey to soak up the golden light and hear nature's noises filling the park. Bring a hat, sunglasses, and sunscreen to protect your skin from the Florida sun.

Airboat tours are more than just a tourist attraction; they are a one-of-a-kind and exhilarating way to experience the Everglades. So prepare to embark on an unforgettable vacation!

Nine Mile Pond Canoe Trail

Imagine yourself smoothly navigating a maze of towering mangroves, with sunlight filtering through the green foliage and the soothing sound of your paddle breaking the perfect silence. Herein lies the fascination of the Nine Mile Pond Canoe Trail, a hidden gem in the heart of Everglades National Park.

This course is about 5.2 miles long and offers a range of paddling opportunities. Strange mangrove islands cast complicated shadows, little green marshes teeming with life, and even a tiny, winding stream full of wonders waiting to be uncovered. Keep an eye out for a variety of species flying above, including otters playing in the river and alligators sunbathing on the banks.

Nine Mile Pond gives more than just breathtaking beauty; it also offers an insight into the vulnerable Everglades ecosystem. Remember while you paddle that you are traveling through an important habitat for a variety of creatures. Discover how mangrove forests, sawgrass grasslands, and the life they sustain are all delicately balanced. Reduce your impact, be a responsible visitor, and leave just footprints (or paddle strokes!).

The best time to explore the Nine Mile Pond Canoe Trail is in the fall and winter, when the water levels are at their peak. Remember that this is a backcountry trail, so pack light and carry food, water, sunscreen, and insect spray. If you don't have your own kayaks or canoes, you may hire them at the Flamingo Marina.

More than simply a place to paddle quietly, the Nine Mile Pond Canoe Trail allows people to connect with nature, detach from everyday life, and create lifetime memories. Take your paddle and enjoy the quiet for an unforgettable excursion in the heart of the Everglades!

Consider going on a canoe trip with competent naturalists. They will not only point out hidden jewels and ensure a pleasurable and safe experience, but they will also provide valuable insights into the ecology.

Take note that the Everglades' ecosystem is vulnerable. Pay attention to your actions, respect the animals, and leave no trace. Let us work together to safeguard this natural wonder for future generations to enjoy.

Ranger-Led Programs

Experience the Everglades with enlightening, engaging ranger-led programs instead of just passive gazing! These encounters go deeper than the surface, revealing mysteries and enhancing your knowledge of this amazing environment.

Tailored to Your Interests: There is a program for everyone, be it an avid birdwatcher, inquisitive naturalist, or someone looking for an immersed experience. Options include stargazing canoe expeditions, narrated treks through cypress swamps, and evening presentations with fascinating local history.

Behind the Scenes Access: Come along with park rangers, the real Everglades stewards, and learn insider secrets. Discover intriguing information about the park's residents, from secretive panthers to endangered manatees, by posing questions and exploring the park's past. You could even be able to take part in citizen science initiatives or observe active conservation activities.

Learn Interactively: Programs taught by rangers are lively experiences rather than dry lectures. Alivening the Everglades with narrative, interactive activities, and demonstrations is what to expect. Find out what animals have left behind, discover the purposes of local plants, or take in the eerie sounds of nocturnal animals by night.

A Deeper Connection: Develop a relationship with the Everglades that goes beyond the picture-perfect landscapes. These initiatives motivate people to take action to save the ecosystem by fostering an appreciation for its fragile balance. Go away having gained fresh insight into the complex dance between the effects of humans and the environment.

Pick Your Own Adventure: You're likely to discover a program that fits your interests and schedule among the many that are offered all year long. Make reservations in advance, especially during the busiest times of the year, and check park websites or visitor centers for current options.

Keep in mind that events hosted by rangers are not only educational but also life-changing. To discover the actual wonder of the Everglades, put down your guidebook and go hiking with a ranger!

Anhinga Trail

Want to see some of the vibrant life of the Everglades without venturing too deep into the backcountry? glimpse no farther than the Anhinga Trail, a short but captivating circuit that provides an up-close glimpse at the park's diverse occupants.

This 0.8-mile trail through sawgrass prairie and freshwater slough is paved, readily accessible, and abundant in wildlife. Be aware of the namesake anhingas, whose long necks penetrate the water in pursuit of unsuspecting prey. Turtles sunbathe on rocks, alligators bask on sun-drenched logs, and singing fills the air. If you look closely, you may see the elusive bobcat and even timid raccoons hidden in the underbrush.

Instead of only witnessing species, the Anhinga Trail's ultimate purpose is to engage you in the rhythm of the Everglades. Listen to the trickling water in the slough, inhale the earthy perfume of the wetlands, and feel the mild air whisper through the sawgrass. You'll feel relaxed and connected to the natural environment long after you've walked this path.

Although there is always the possibility of seeing animals along this popular path, the best times to do so are in the early morning or late afternoon when the temperature is cool. Don't forget to bring your camera, comfortable shoes, and sunscreen/bug repellant! Remember, this is a guest article on an endangered ecosystem. Follow the track, avoid disturbing the animals, and leave no trace.

The Everglades provide considerably more than what the Anhinga Trail can deliver. After your walk, visit the neighboring Royal Palm Visitor Center to learn more about the park's unique environment and conservation programs. Following your visit, you may be compelled to discover more about the riches of this unique setting, which may serve as a springboard for future inquiry.

Step onto the Anhinga Trail and allow nature to tickle your interest. To guarantee that this natural treasure is conserved for future generations, remember that responsible tourism and environmental stewardship are required.

Hiking & Biking Trails

Absolutely, the following list includes some of Everglades National Park's top hiking and bike routes:

- **Anhinga Trail:** One of the park's most well-liked paths, measuring 0.8 miles, is this paved loop path. There are birds, alligators, and other species to be seen as you traverse through a verdant cypress swamp. With breathtaking views of the Everglades, the Anhinga route Observation Tower is also located along the route.
- **Shark Valley Tram Tour:** Alligators, birds, and other animals may be seen on this 15-mile tram journey that passes through the center of the Everglades. Along with its breathtaking views of the Everglades, the Shark Valley Observation Tower is another stop on the trip.

- **Long Pine Key Nature Trail:** You may observe a variety of trees, plants, and animals on this 0.8-mile circular walk, which winds through a hardwood hammock. Along the walk is the Long Pine Key Observation Tower, which provides views of Florida Bay and the Everglades.

- **Gumbo Limbo Trail:** You may witness a variety of trees, plants, and animals on this 0.4-mile boardwalk walkway that winds through a mangrove forest. Along the Gumbo Limbo Trail is the Gumbo Limbo Trail Observation Tower, which provides views of Florida Bay and the Everglades.

- **Mahogany Hammock Trail:** This 0.5-mile circular walk leads through a hardwood hammock, home to a wide range of flora and fauna. The Mahogany Hammock route Observation Tower, which provides views of

Florida Bay and the Everglades, is also located along the route.

These are only a handful of the numerous fantastic hiking and bike routes found in the National Park of Everglades. Your fitness level, your hobbies, and the season you will be traveling should all be considered while making travel plans. There's an excellent trail discovery tool on the park website to help you focus.

Apart from the aforementioned pathways, there are other alternative routes for biking exploration inside the Everglades. One option would be to hire a bike and ride the Tamiami Trail, which passes through the park. Another option is to go on a guided bike trip, which is a fantastic opportunity to discover the park's hidden treasures.

The Everglades is an incredibly wonderful and unique area, no matter how you decide to experience it. It is a site you will never forget because of its varied ecosystems, an abundance of species, and breathtaking beauty.

Tips for hiking and biking in Everglades National Park:

- Put on loose-fitting shoes and rags to cover up.
- Bring lots of water and sunblock with you.
- Be mindful of your surroundings and keep an eye out for any wildlife.
- Avoid disturbing the flora or fauna by staying on the designated pathways.
- Leave no trace at all. Remove all of your possessions and rubbish.

Flamingo Visitor Center

Flamingo Visitor Center, located away at the southernmost point of the Everglades, is more than simply a place to halt; it's a starting point for exploration and education. Think of:

Views from Above: Take in the immensity before you dive in. Reach the summit of the viewing tower to see the Everglades spread out in front of you, a mosaic of mangrove forests, shimmering water, and sawgrass grasslands. The scene is ready for your investigation with this amazing viewpoint.

Interactive Exhibits: Discover the complex biosphere of the Everglades. Explore the undiscovered beauties of the mangrove ecosystem, interact with lifelike alligator models, and hear wading bird cries. The park's varied population and fragile balance are brought to life through interactive exhibits.

Professional Perspectives: Utilize the expertise of park rangers. Participate in educational activities, take guided tours, or ask questions. Find more about the Everglades' past, present, and particular difficulties that this important environment faces.

Gateway to Exploration: The Flamingo Visitor Center serves as your adventure's launching pad. Select your next adventure, pick up maps, and hire canoes or kayaks. Take a boat excursion for amazing animal encounters, hike through secret paths, or experience an exhilarating airboat ride.

A Window into the Past: Explore the rich history of the park through A Window into the Past. Discover the Tequesta people, who were the first people to live in the Everglades, by looking through the historical displays. Learn about their struggles and special connection to this place.

Beyond the Center: Flamingo serves as a gathering place for a variety of events. Fish in the crystal-clear lakes, kayak along the serene canals, or set up camp beneath the starry sky. Recall that the Everglades are a living museum; please take care of the ecosystem and leave no trace.

The Flamingo Visitor Center provides a window into the essence of the Everglades, not merely a place to start. Come experience this amazing environment, learn about it, and make lifelong memories by connecting with it.

Experiencing the Everglades Beyond the Park

Miami

Miami is a dynamic metropolis that teems with excitement and vitality. This location offers the opportunity to enjoy the sun on immaculate beaches, take in the striking Art Deco architecture, and fully immerse oneself in a multicultural environment.

Miami has something for everyone, whether your goal is to experience a spectacular night out, a dose of creative expression, or a taste of different cultures.

Take a stroll around Miami's Art Deco neighborhood and transport yourself to the opulent 1930s. Bright avenues like Collins Avenue and Ocean Drive are lined with pastel-hued buildings with geometric designs and chrome accents. You may either take pictures and enjoy the striking surroundings or go on a guided tour to discover more about the architectural significance and history of this distinctive design.

Miami's nightlife comes to life as the sun sets. Every taste may be satisfied by a variety of venues, from underground speakeasies in Wynwood to vibrant dance clubs in South Beach. Dance the night away to live music in Little Havana, enjoy well made drinks on a rooftop bar with a view of the city, or see a top-tier DJ performance at a prestigious club.

Due to the city's varied population, Miami's food culture is just as lively as its nightlife and art. Taste real Cuban food in Little Havana, treat yourself to fresh seafood at a restaurant by the bay, or take a gastronomic trip around the world by sampling Ethiopian food in Little Ethiopia or Haitian food in Little Haiti. Make sure to try some delectable regional dishes.

Even while Miami Beach is undoubtedly glitzy and glamorous, you might find hidden gems by going off the well-traveled road. Take a leisurely stroll through the tranquil Vizcaya Museum and Gardens, peruse the chic Wynwood stores and art galleries, or spend a day excursion to the Florida Keys to experience an island getaway.

Miami's warm atmosphere is a testament to its embracing of diversity. You'll discover a welcoming atmosphere where everyone feels at home, whether you're traveling alone, with friends, or with family.

Thus, prepare to make lifelong memories in this vibrant city by packing your luggage, embracing Miami's beat, and getting ready.

Florida Keys

Think of brilliant coral reefs brimming with colorful fish, sugar-white sand beaches, and the relaxed island atmosphere of the Florida Keys. This breathtaking archipelago, which stretches south from Florida's mainland, offers adventurers and lovers of the great outdoors an incredible getaway.

Island Hopping Bliss: Explore this 120-mile chain by jumping about and taking in each key's own appeal. John Pennekamp Coral Reef State Park at Key Largo, known as the "Diving Capital of the World," beckons with its underwater experiences. With the opportunity to catch marlin, tarpon, and other species, Islamorada, known as the "Sport Fishing Capital of the World," lures fishermen. The "Family Islands," Marathon, is renowned for its immaculate beaches, chance to see dolphins, and relaxed island lifestyle. Lastly, Key West, the southernmost tip of the US mainland, is a dynamic hub of historical charm, nightlife, and sunsets.

Explore a Marine Wonderland: The Florida Keys are home to an amazing undersea realm that lies beyond the shores. Paddle a kayak through glistening clean seas and see playful dolphins and stately manatees. Discover colorful coral reefs when snorkeling or scuba diving, where you may come across parrotfish, angelfish, and perhaps even sea turtles. Take a glass-bottom boat excursion to witness the underwater extravaganza without getting wet for an absolutely exhilarating experience.

Beyond the Beaches: The Florida Keys have more to offer than simply sun and beach. Go Beyond the Beaches. Wander through luxuriant mangrove woods that are home to a diverse range of birds and habitats. Discover historical locations that provide breathtaking vistas and an insight into the past of the islands, such as Fort Zachary Taylor Historic State Park. Savor delicious seafood delicacies and lively art scenes in every key as you fully immerse yourself in the native way of life.

A Universal Heaven: The Florida Keys provide experiences for all types of travelers, including heart-pounding adventures, tranquil beach getaways, and opportunities to get back in touch with nature. So grab your sunhat, swimwear, and spirit of exploration, and get ready to be mesmerized by this island paradise's beauty and enchantment.

Remind yourself to be mindful of the delicate maritime ecosystem. Avoid handling coral, use sunscreen that is safe for reefs, and dispose of rubbish properly. Let's preserve the Florida Keys' natural state for future generations.

Key West

Forget the US mainland; hear murmurs of pirates, conch shells, and mojitos made in the style of Hemingway from Key West. The southernmost point of the nation, this lively island provides a special fusion of charm and history, making it ideal for your next journey.

Southernmost Charm: The fragrance of fresh seafood drifting from lively cafés, palm palms swinging in the mild wind, and pastel-colored conch cottages dotting tiny alleys are all examples of Southernmost Charm. Key West invites you to calm down and enjoy the small things in life with its laid-back island ambiance. Wander Duval Street, the center of the excitement, with its eclectic stores, fun bars, and street entertainers. Unwind on Sunset Pier while the sun sets and the sky bursts into brilliant hues.

Rich History Whispers: Explore the island's past, from its origins as a pirate sanctuary to its literary heritage. At his house and museum, follow along Ernest Hemingway's footsteps and imagine him writing his classic tales. At Fort Zachary Taylor, take a step back in time and see its guns from the American Civil War defending the shore. Discover the rich cultural fabric of the island at the Key West Art & Historical Society and the Mel Fisher

Maritime Heritage Museum, where you may unearth artifacts recovered from shipwrecks.

Unusual Adventures Await: There is much in Key West for every adventurer to enjoy, even beyond simply soaking up the ambiance. Discover vivid coral reefs and lively dolphins as you kayak through mangrove forests and crystal-clear waterways. Sail at dusk, enjoying the cool air and watching playful dolphins against the backdrop of the blazing sky. Explore shipwrecks and a plethora of colorful marine life while diving into history in a glass-bottom boat.

Embrace the Quirky: The quirks of Key West are what make it so vibrant. See the buoy at Southernmost Point, which represents the symbolic border of the United States. Take in the vibrant street show "Sunset Celebration" with music, juggling, and dramatic fireworks at Mallory Square.

Take part in the lively "Duval Crawl," a pub crawl with a holiday twist, and enjoy beverages at famous establishments while taking in the energetic nightlife.

Key West is an experience as much as a place. Discover the enchantment of its vibrant streets, immerse yourself in its extensive past, and embrace the relaxed island way of life. So be ready to be mesmerized by Key West's enchantment, pack your luggage and bring your spirit of exploration.

Honor the distinctive culture and nature of the island. Take care while disposing of rubbish, pay attention to wildlife, and enjoy the relaxed island lifestyle. Let us preserve the beauty of Key West for future generations.

Making Memories that Last

Capturing the Beauty

The Everglades entices photographers with its unadulterated beauty and varied animals. It is a patchwork of sawgrass grasslands, mangrove forests, and shimmering rivers. Here are some pointers and undiscovered talents to improve your photos:

Embrace the Golden Hours: The Everglades are magically lit up at dawn and dusk. Arrange your trips to take pictures of the sky exploding with hues, reflecting on placid bodies of water, or creating striking shadows on cypress knees.

Beyond Alligators: The Everglades have more to offer than just the famous reptiles! Look for the brilliant feathers of wading birds, the elusive bobcat patrolling the plains, or the ancient allure of turtles lounging on logs. The fine features of flowers and insects may be seen through macro photography.

Compose with Intent: Utilize foreground objects like grasses or branches to frame your topic. Look for fascinating patterns in the foliage, leading lines in trails, and reflections in the water. To accentuate the solitude and beauty of your topic, embrace negative space.

Embrace Different Perspective: Climb an observation tower for sweeping views, or go low to capture the immensity of the sawgrass grasslands. Embrace Different Perspectives. Be creative and don't be scared to use waterproof covers for underwater photography or drone photography as long as you go by park restrictions.

Accept the Unexpected: Be ready for unanticipated events. For far-off wildlife and expansive vistas, bring a wide-angle lens and a telephoto lens. Keep glare reducers on hand, and try slow shutter speeds for surreal water effects.

Recognize that you are a visitor to this fragile environment and treat it with respect. Use natural light wherever feasible, keep your influence to a minimum, and don't disturb wildlife. Recall that often the most memorable pictures are the ones you take but don't have a chance to snap.

Embark on a trip or workshop with local photographers. Get tips on where to shoot, learn how to shoot in the Everglades specifically, and receive insightful criticism on your work.

Discover the hidden wonders of the Everglades. With your camera, a feeling of amazement, and these pointers in hand, get ready to capture the essence of this special habitat with every shot.

Unwinding & Connecting with Nature

In the Everglades National Park, get away from the daily grind and rediscover the embrace of Discover the embrace of nature in the Everglades National Park and get away from the daily grind. Let this be a voyage of inner serenity and profound connection rather than merely sightseeing.

Breathe in the clean, humid air, and listen to the sound of rustling leaves and chirping as you become fully submerged in tranquility. Walk along quiet paths while taking in the soft ground beneath your feet and the sun's rays filtering through the trees. Paddling a kayak across calm rivers, you may take your time seeing the sights. Locate a peaceful area and take a seat, allowing the silence and immensity to envelope you.

Disconnect to Reconnect: Put your phone down, turn off your alerts, and take a step away from technology. Get in touch with your senses again and take in the sights, sounds, and scents that surround you. Take note of a spiderweb's minute intricacies, a butterfly's graceful dance, or the clouds' captivating patterns against the clear blue sky.

Awaken your Senses: In order to awaken your senses, take part in mindful exercises like yoga or meditation in a natural setting. Pay attention to your breathing and the rise and fall of your chest in harmony with the surrounding environment. Let yourself be drawn into the present moment by the sounds of the Everglades.

Starry Night Spectacle: Take in the Everglades' amazing enchantment while they are blanketed with stars. Step away from the light pollution and take in the breathtaking view of the Milky Way on the black canvas. Hear the nighttime lullaby of the wildness itself, performed by owls, insects, and frogs.

Accept Thankfulness: Consider the wonder and vulnerability of this biosphere. Savor the little things in life, like the taste of fresh water, the warmth of the sun, and a refreshing wind on your skin. Develop an attitude of gratitude for your position in this special atmosphere.

Take Only Memories, Leave Only Footprints: When you go, leave no trace behind. Reduce your influence while honoring the Everglades' fragile ecosystem and fauna. Recall that genuine connection to nature requires care and responsibility.

Let the Everglades be your peaceful retreat where you can relax, get back in touch with yourself, and discover serenity in the middle of the nature. You'll go on an amazing journey of revitalization and renewal if you have an open mind and an appreciative heart.

Sharing Your Experience

Once you exit the park, your Everglades experience continues. Share your experience and encourage others to conserve this special environment to become an advocate for it. Here's how to do it:

Capture & Post: Use pertinent hashtags, such as #EvergladesNationalPark and #ProtectOurEverglades, when posting your gorgeous images and videos to social media. Showcase the park's diversity and beauty in your images to pique viewers' interest and encourage exploration.

Become a Storyteller: Develop Your Narrative Skills by Composing a blog piece or travelog that describes your adventures, the marvels you saw, and the difficulties the Everglades faces. Provide personal tales, travel advice, and connections to environmental advocacy groups.

Educate & Advocate: Discuss the Everglades with friends, family, and coworkers. Talk about fascinating facts, bust myths, and emphasize how crucial it is to preserve this unique habitat. Urge them to visit sensibly and back environmental initiatives.

Support Conservation: Contribute to respectable groups that are defending the Everglades to show your support for conservation. Give your time to citizen science projects, educational events, and park cleanups. No matter how small or large, every gift counts.

Minimize Your Impact: Lead a sustainable lifestyle. Minimize your carbon footprint, use less water, and use environmentally friendly items. Recall that preserving the Everglades begins at home.

Provide advice on responsible travel when visiting the Everglades. By booking eco-friendly lodging, showing consideration for animals, and abiding by park rules, you may urge others to lessen their own effect.

Exhibit Passion: Your zealous energy is infectious! Tell everyone you know how much you like the Everglades. Motivate people to take care of the environment by supporting its preservation and making sure that its beauty lasts for future generations.

Recall that even little things can have far-reaching effects. Through sharing your story and encouraging others to take action, you can become a force for change and guarantee that the Everglades will continue to be a dynamic natural treasure for many years to come.

Safety & Sustainability

Respecting Wildlife & Their Habitat

From recognizable alligators to elusive panthers, the Everglades are teeming with amazing life. Remind yourself that you are a guest in their home when you set off on your excursion. Here are some tips for making sure everyone has a polite and enjoyable experience:

Admire from a distance: Fight the want to approach too closely to animals. To view them without interfering with their normal activity, keep a safe distance using binoculars or telephoto lenses. Keep in mind that overtures that appear innocuous may be interpreted as threats.

Remain At a Safe Distance: Avoid feeding or handling untamed animals. While touching can spread disease and cause discomfort, offering food interferes with their normal eating habits and hunting instincts. Allow them to mingle and forage as nature meant.

Leave No Trace: Empty your possessions and all rubbish. Leave nothing behind that might endanger wildlife or contaminate the ecosystem, including food waste and wrappers. To lessen your influence, adhere to the "leave no trace" philosophy.

Remain on Designated Trails: To prevent uprooting delicate plants and upsetting nesting habitats, stay on designated trails. Allow the species to continue living in peace and harmony in these secret places.

Silent Observation: Reduce loud noises and steer clear of abrupt movements. Move slowly and speak quietly to avoid frightening animals by giving them time to become used to your presence. Recall that those who approach the Everglades with care and respect can unlock its mysteries.

Recognize Your Environment: Take care where you walk and don't mess with any burrows or nests. When you come across an animal on the route, gently move aside and give them space. You shouldn't have to change their house to fit you in.

Be an Advocate: Tell people about your polite interactions with animals. Urge children to behave responsibly and to report any instances in which they witness someone endangering wildlife or its natural environment. There is power in your voice.

Being an aware visitor helps maintain a healthy environment and guarantees that future generations can enjoy the Everglades' beauty. Remember that treating the amazing wildlife that calls this region home with care is the cornerstone of an exciting and wonderful journey for both of you.

Sun Protection & Hydration

Florida's subtropical temperature necessitates preparedness, even though the Everglades entice you with its colorful vistas and varied animals. Here's how to keep safe and energized in the heat and sunshine:

Sun Shield Savior: 30 minutes prior to leaving, pack broad-spectrum sunscreen with an SPF of 30 or more and apply liberally (don't forget to cover your ears, lips, and tips of your feet!). Particularly after swimming or perspiring, reapply every two hours. For further protection, think about wearing clothes with broad brims on hats, long sleeves, and slacks.

Hydration Hero: Throughout the Everglades, water is your greatest ally. Carry a lot of reusable bottles (avoid single-use plastics!) and make sure you drink frequently throughout the day, even if you're not really thirsty. Water should be prioritized above sugary drinks since the heat and humidity can cause dehydration rapidly. For longer walks or hot weather, think about electrolyte-infused products.

Seek Shade Sanctuary: The noon sun may be rather harsh, so look for a shaded area. Arrange your activities so that you may take rests in the shade and hide behind trees, pavilions, or tourist centers. Bring along an umbrella for last-minute shade options.

Mosquito Militia: Although they are not as prevalent as in other tropical areas, mosquitoes may still be found in the Everglades. Apply insect repellent to exposed skin by carefully following the directions on the package, making sure it contains at least 20% DEET. When sleeping outside, take into consideration mosquito netting.

Clothing Selections: Choose airy, light garments composed of natural fibers, such as linen or cotton. Choose loose-fitting clothing to improve air circulation and stay away from heat-attracting dark hues. Carry layers that can dry quickly in case of spills or sudden immersion in water.

Pay Attention to Your Body: It's Important to Take Breaks During Strenuous Activities. If you feel too hot, look for cool places to stay, such as tourist centers or covered areas. Take note of your body's cues and modify your speed accordingly to avoid overexerting yourself.

You can make sure your Everglades journey is full of sunlight, safety, and treasured memories by adhering to these easy suggestions. As always, being ready is essential to fully taking in the park's natural treasures!

Leaving No Trace

Discover the splendors of the Everglades National Park, a diverse landscape with mangrove forests, sawgrass plains, and abundant animals. To ensure that this environment continues to flourish for future generations, it is important to practice responsible tourism. How to ensure that your Everglades expedition leaves just footprints (and maybe a few unforgettable memories)

Pack the Essentials for "Leave No Trace": Consider more than just sunscreen and a swimsuit. Bring a "wag bag" for your pet's waste, cloth bags, and reusable water bottles. To prevent endangering wildlife and damaging the fragile ecosystem, dispose of all waste appropriately in the specified containers.

Follow the Path, Don't Forge Your Own Path: Refrain from straying from the prescribed routes. Damage to delicate ecosystems and animal habitats results from trampling plants. Follow well-trod paths and take in the view from a distance. Recall that the Everglades are a living museum, and we are but visitors.

The wildlife are not intended for your selfie, so treat it with respect: Never feed, pursue, or bother animals. Use your zoom lens rather than your flash and keep a safe distance away from them. Recall that these are not props for photos, but really wild animals. Their natural behavior—rather than our amusement—is what determines their existence.

Reduce Your Impact: Whenever practical, choose environmentally friendly modes of transportation like bicycles or canoes. Use reusable water bottles and take shorter showers to save water. Consider your volume and give the sounds of nature more prominence. To preserve this priceless environment, every little action matters.

Turn Become an Advocate and Share Your Story: Get the word out about eco-friendly travel methods! Emphasize the value of preserving the Everglades by showing your friends and family your experiences and pictures. Urge people to take care of this natural wonder by encouraging them to "leave no trace" and act as conscientious stewards.

Being a responsible tourist means honoring the environment, the people who live there, and the fragile ecosystem of the Everglades. Take off with awe in mind, walk carefully, and depart from the Everglades with color.

Tips and Recommendations

A spectacular natural marvel, Everglades National Park provides visitors with a unique and varied experience. To help you make the most of your visit, consider the following advice and suggestions:

1. Timing: Schedule your trip between November and April, the dry season, to escape the intense heat and bugs. Both the weather and the fauna are nice and more active.

2. wildlife Viewing: To photograph the amazing animals, carry a camera and binoculars. To see alligators, manatees, turtles, and a variety of bird species, including herons and egrets, take a guided boat trip.

3. Hiking Trails: Take a stroll along the park's trails, which include the Gumbo Limbo and Anhinga trails. You may experience the distinctive sawgrass marshes, cypress trees, and bromeliads of the Everglades by following these trails.

4. Canoeing and kayaking: Take a trip around the park's rivers by renting a canoe or kayak. A distinct viewpoint of the Everglades is offered by the tranquility, which permits intimate interactions with animals.

5. Ranger-led events: Take part in events, seminars, and nighttime walks conducted by rangers. The park's history, ecology, and conservation initiatives are all highlighted by these educational opportunities.

6. Mosquito Protection: Use insect repellent and wear lightweight, long-sleeved clothes if you want to avoid being bothered by mosquitoes. If possible, try to camp under appropriate netting or remain in screened-in lodging.

7. Safety Precautions: Avert alligator habitats, observe animals from a distance, and stick to approved pathways. To guarantee your safety and the preservation of this fragile environment, abide by the park's laws and regulations.

You'll have an amazing day exploring the Everglades National Park, learning about its amazing biodiversity, and taking in all of its natural marvels if you heed this advice.

Itinerary

Day 1: Arrival & Immerse in the Mangroves

- **Morning:** Get information and pick up your annual pass for Everglades National Park when you arrive at the Homestead Visitor Center. Refuel in Homestead with a locally sourced breakfast.

- **Afternoon:** Take a hike along the colorful Anhinga Trail, which is home to many birds and reptiles. See alligators and wading birds in their native environment by taking an exhilarating airboat trip in Shark Valley.

- **Evening:** Get comfortable with your Everglades City lodging. Enjoy a fantastic supper that highlights regional cuisine from the Florida Keys while unwinding beneath the clear night sky.

Day 2: Deep Dive into the Wilderness

- **Morning:** On the Nine Mile Pond Canoe Trail, rent kayaks or sign up for a guided canoe trip to explore the ecosystem's hidden treasures while cruising through verdant mangrove woods.
- **Lunch:** Savor a picnic lunch in the middle of the wilderness while taking in the Everglades' music. For amazing sweeping views, go to the neighboring observation tower.
- **Afternoon:** Travel to the park's southernmost location, the Flamingo Visitor Center. Take a boat journey into the isolated wilderness to discover secret mangrove islands and abundant animals while learning about the distinctive ecology of the Florida Keys.
- **Evening:** Visit the Everglades National Park Museum to fully immerse yourself in the

local culture, or go to Everglades City, a neighboring hamlet.

Day 3: Backcountry Exploration & Local Culture

- **Morning:** Take a guided backcountry trek in Shark Valley to begin your day, exploring the interior of the Everglades and discovering the intricate balance of its ecosystems.
- **Lunch:** Enjoy a picnic lunch in the gorgeous outdoors to refuel.
- **Afternoon:** Discover about the customs and ties to the Everglades of the Miccosukee Tribe by visiting the Billie Swamp Safari. Another option is to go to the Big Cypress National Preserve, where you may explore the cypress swamp and look for rare species.

- **Evening:** Admire the vivid hues painting the sky while taking in the day's experiences on an Everglades City sunset cruise.

Day 4: Nature Trails & Hidden Gems

- **Morning:** Explore the Gumbo Limbo Trail to learn about the park's cultural significance and its varied plant life. For beautiful scenery and a taste of backcountry camping, stop at Long Pine Key Campground.
- **Lunch:** Enjoy a typical lunch in Everglades City while taking in the vibes of the community.
- **Afternoon:** Take a bike ride along the picturesque Snake Bight Trail to experience the fresh air and various sceneries. Alternatively, explore the tranquil Turner

River Mangrove Maze by kayak to discover undiscovered gems and a variety of marine species.

- **Evening:** As you unwind at your lodging, consider the various experiences you've had during your trip to the Everglades.

Day 5: Farewell & Lasting Memories

- **Morning:** Take a lovely drive down the Tamiami Trail, pausing at the Coastal Prairie Trail to get one last look at the various ecosystems found inside the park.
- **Lunch:** Savor a delectable lunch of locally caught seafood while taking in the beachside ambience in Key Largo.
- **Afternoon:** Optional: Take a snorkeling or diving tour of John Pennekamp Coral Reef

State Park to discover the underwater treasures of the Florida Keys. As an alternative, unwind on the sand while cherishing your memories and soaking in the sun.

- Evening: As you leave with a greater understanding of the Everglades' exceptional marvels, think back on your incredible journey there, knowing that you helped to preserve it.

Keep in mind that you may alter this schedule to suit your tastes and interests; it's only a suggestion. If you embrace the spirit of exploration, the Everglades will undoubtedly leave you with unforgettable experiences!

CONCLUSION

It's time to say goodbye to our amazing swamp tour through Everglades National Park, gator fans! By now, you should be able to handle the sawgrass prairies like a swamp explorer with years of experience, recognize more animals than Steve Irwin (hopefully without the khakis!), and possibly even impress your friends with some truly amazing Everglades lore.

But don't panic, this is only a "see you later" rather than an actual departure. This excellent booklet may be used on more than one swamp safari. Stash it in your backpack, use it to create lively pre-trip planning sessions, or just flip the pages to relive the magic whenever you need a little sunshine and swamp spirit.

Always remember that the Everglades are a living, breathing habitat, so leave just your footprints (or maybe some canoe paddle marks). And, hey, feel free to counsel any perplexed tourist you come across who is stammering about "dang mosquitoes" while pacing in circles. After all, even in the swamp, sharing is caring!

Thank you for making this guidebook your swamp side buddy, from the bottom of my heart as an Everglades enthusiast. May your life be filled with unforgettable events, one-of-a-kind animal encounters, and minimal mosquito bites. Now go out and discover new things, have fun, and remember that the only bad day in the Everglades is one spent indoors!

Made in the USA
Columbia, SC
25 September 2024

43043608R00061